THE COMPLETE PIANO PLAYER COLLECTION
BOOK 3

Wise Publications
London/New York/Sydney/Cologne

Exclusive Distributors:
Music Sales Limited
78 Newman Street, London W1P 3LA, England.
Music Sales Pty. Limited
27 Clarendon Street, Artarmon, Sydney, NSW 2064, Australia.

This book © Copyright 1985 by
Wise Publications
ISBN 0.7119.0668.8
Order No. AM 39603

Music Sales complete catalogue lists thousands of
titles and is free from your local music book shop,
or direct from Music Sales Limited.
Please send 25p in stamps for postage to
Music Sales Limited, 78 Newman Street, London W1P 3LA.

Printed in England by
The Camelot Press Limited, Southampton.

FOLK SONGS

The Foggy, Foggy Dew

When I was a bach'lor, I lived all alone,
I worked at the weaver's trade;
And the only, only thing I did that was wrong,
Was to woo a fair young maid.
I woo'd her in the winter time
And in the summer, too;
And the only, only thing I did that was wrong,
Was to keep her from the foggy, foggy dew.

American

Not too slow

Peter Gray

Once on a time there lived a man, his name was Peter Gray.
He lived way down in that 'ere town called Pennsylvan-i-a.
Blow ye winds of morning, blow ye winds, heigh ho!
Blow ye winds of morning, blow, blow, blow!

American

*Certain fingerings of special import have been circled to
bring them more forcefully to the students attention.

The Drunken Sailor

What shall we do with the drunken sailor,
What shall we do with the drunken sailor,
What shall we do with the drunken sailor,
Earlye in the morning?

Hooray and up she rises,
Hooray and up she rises,
Hooray and up she rises,
Earlye in the morning!

Sea Chantey

Rather lively

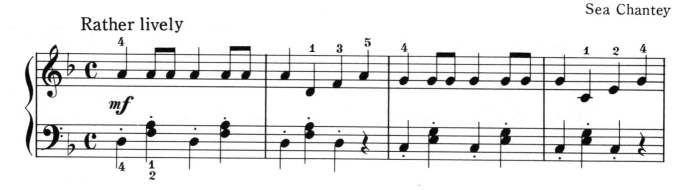

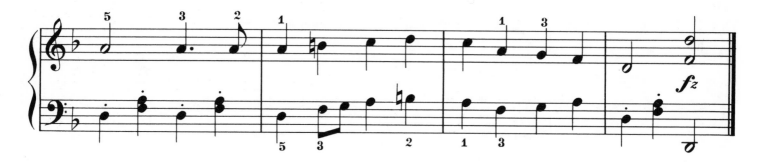

When Love Is Kind

When love is kind,
Cheerful and free,
Love's sure to find
Welcome from me!

Old English Air

Not too slow

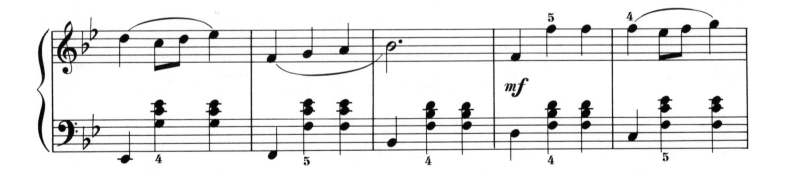

Alouette

Alouette, gentille alouette,
Alouette, je te plumerai.
Je te plumerai la tête,
Je te plumerai la tête,
Et la tête,
Et la tête,
Alouette, gentille alouette,
Alouette, je te plumerai.

French Canadian

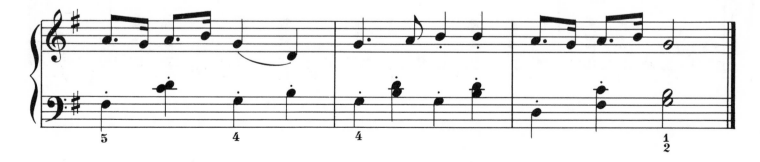

Variation

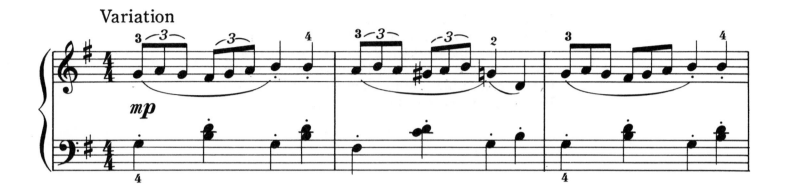

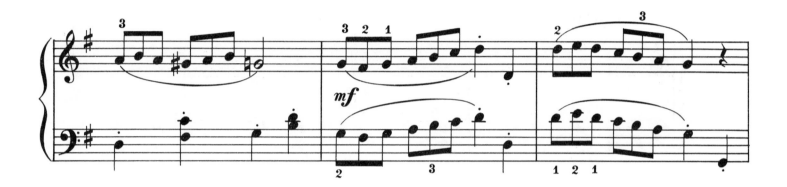

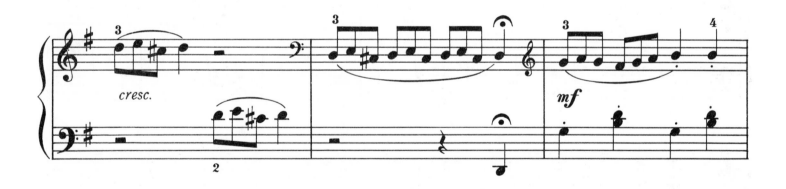

I Ride An Old Paint

I ride an old Paint, I lead an old Dan,
I'm goin' to Montan' for to throw the hoolihan.
They feed in the coulees, they water in the draw,
Their tails are all matted, their backs are all raw.
Ride around, little dogies, ride around them slow,
For the fiery and snuffy are a-rarin' to go.

American

The Rio Grande

Oh say, were you ever in Rio Grande?
    Way, oh Rio.
It's there that the river flows down golden sand.
    And we're bound for the Rio Grande.
Then away, love, away.
    Way, oh Rio.
So fare ye well, my pretty young girl,
    For we're bound for the Rio Grande.

Sea Chantey

Clementine

In a cavern in a canyon,
Excavating for a mine,
Lived a miner, forty-niner,
And his daughter Clementine.

Oh, my darling, oh, my darling,
Oh, my darling Clementine,
Thou art lost and gone forever,
Dreadful sorry, Clementine.

Rather lively

American

The Three Ravens

There were three Ra'ens, sat on a tree,
   Down a-down, hey downie down,
They were as black as black might be,
   With a down.
The one of them said to his mate,
"Where shall we our breakfast take?"
With a down, derry, derry, derry, down, down.

English

The Little Sailboat

There is a little, little sailboat,
There is a tiny, little sailboat;
And it has ne - ne - never sailed away,
Oh no, it's ne - ne - never sailed away,
Away, away.

French

Sailor's Hornpipe

English Dance

Lively

All Through The Night

Sleep, my child, and peace attend thee
　　All through the night;
Guardian angels God will send thee
　　All through the night.
Soft the drowsy hours are creeping
　　Hill and dale in slumber steeping,
I my loving vigil keeping
　　All through the night.

Welsh

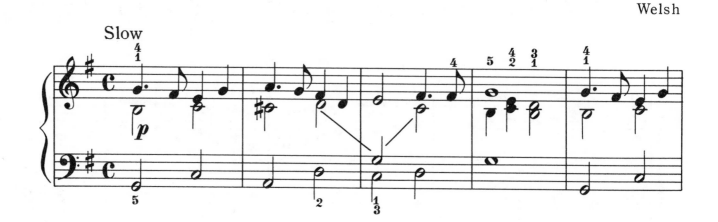

Shenandoah

Oh, Shenandoah, I long to hear you;
Away, you rolling river,
Oh Shenandoah, I long to hear you;
Away, we're bound away,
Across the wide Missouri.

American

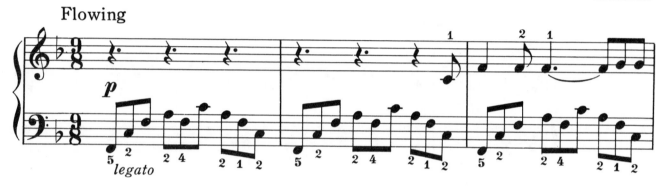

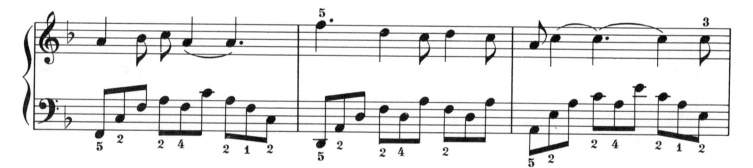

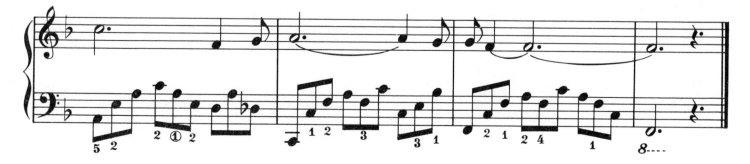

Barbara Allen

In Scarlet town where I was born,
There was a young maid dwellin',
Made every youth cry, "Well-a-day,"
Her name was Barbara Allen.

English

Not too slow

(Bring out the Melody L.H.)

Greensleeves

Alas, my love, you do me wrong
To cast me off discourteously,
And I have loved you so long
Delighting in your company.
Greensleeves was all my joy,
Greensleeves was my delight,
Greensleeves was my heart of gold,
And who but Lady Greensleeves?

English

Rather slow

Hopak

Russian Folk Dance

Very lively

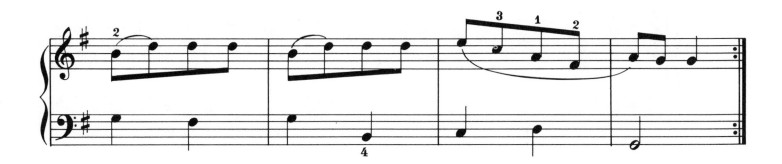

The Last Rose Of Summer

'Tis the last rose of summer,
Left blooming alone;
All her lovely companions
Are faded and gone;
No flow'r of her kindred,
No rosebud is nigh,
To reflect back her blushes,
Or give sigh for sigh!

Irish

Slow and peaceful

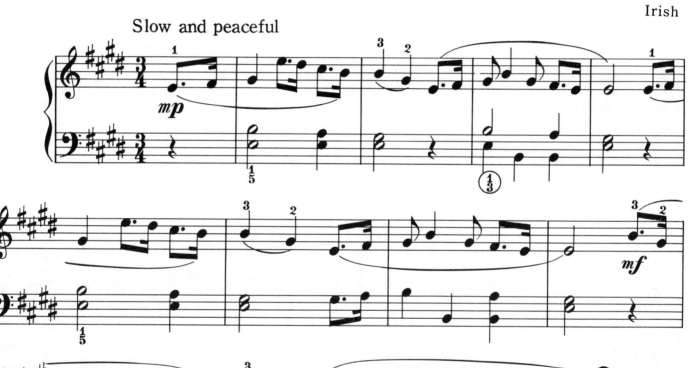

March Of The Three Kings

Provencal Christmas Carol

In march time

SOLOS

Johann Anton André – Bagatelle, 29

Johann Sebastian Bach – Minuet, 25

Johann Sebastian Bach – Minuet, 26

George Becker – Sad Story, 35

Ludwig van Beethoven – Ecossaise, 31

Georges Bizet – Prelude, 37

Edvard Grieg – Grisen, 38

Joseph Haydn – Contredance, 27

Dmitri Kabalevsky – Clowns, 40

Ignaz Moscheles – March, 36

Wolfgang Amadeus Mozart – Allegro, 30

Henry Purcell – Prelude, 24

Alessandro Scarlatti – Aria, 28

Franz Schubert – Ecossaise, 32

Franz Schubert – Waltz, 32

Fritz Spindler – Waltz, 34

Peter I. Tchaikovsky – The Organ Grinder, 39

Georg Philipp Telemann – Gigue, 24

Carl Maria von Weber – German Dance, 33

André, Johann Anton (German) 1775-1842
Bach, Johann Sebastian (German) 1685-1750
Becker, George (German) 1834-1928
Beethoven, Ludwig van (German-Austrian) 1770-1827
Bizet, Georges (French) 1838-1875
Grieg, Edvard (Norwegian) 1843-1907
Haydn, Joseph (Austrian) 1732-1809
Kabalevsky, Dmitri (Russian) 1904-
Moscheles, Ignaz (German) 1794-1870
Mozart, Wolfgang Amadeus (Austrian) 1756-1791
Purcell, Henry (English) 1659-1695
Scarlatti, Alessando (Italian) 1660-1725
Schubert, Franz (Austrian) 1797-1828
Spindler, Fritz (German) 1817-1905
Tchaikovsky, Peter Ilyich (Russian) 1840-1893
Telemann, Georg Philipp (German) 1681-1767
Weber, Carl Maria von (German) 1786-1826

Prelude

Moderato

Henry Purcell

Gigue

Georg Philipp Telemann

Allegro

Minuet

Johann Sebastian Bach

Andante

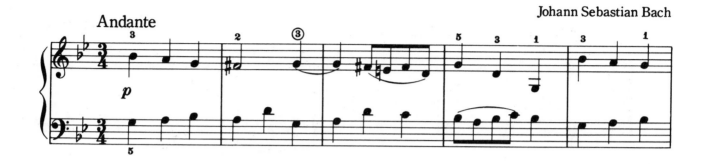

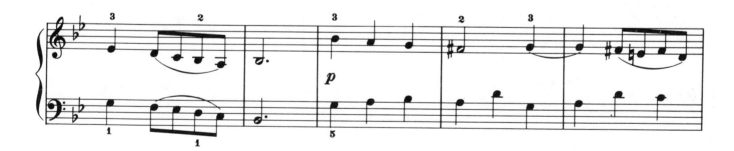

Minuet

Johann Sebastian Bach

Contredance

Allegretto

Joseph Haydn

Aria

Alessandro Scarlatti

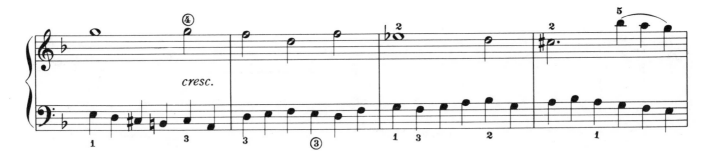

Bagatelle

Johann Anton André

Andantino con grazia

Allegro

Wolfgang Amadeus Mozart

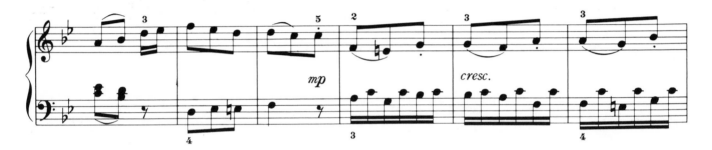

Ecossaise

Allegretto

Ludwig van Beethoven

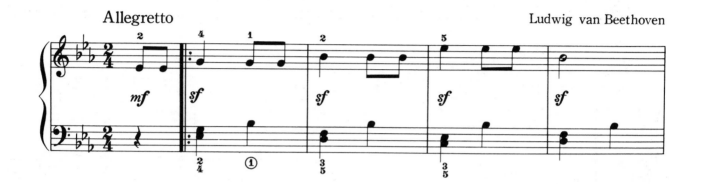

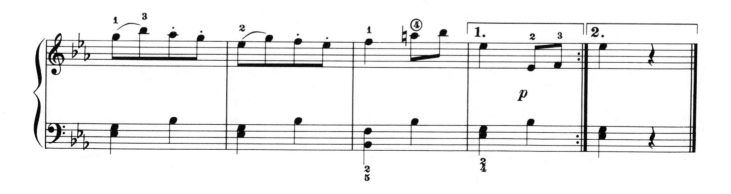

Ecossaise

Allegretto

Franz Schubert

Waltz

Franz Schubert

Moderato

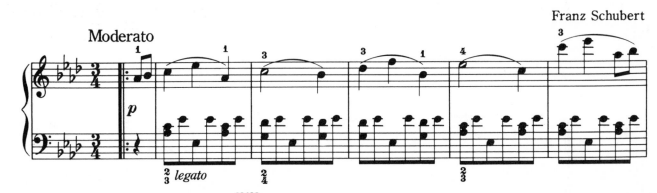

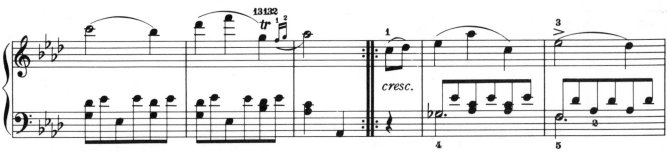

German Dance

Carl Maria von Weber

Allegretto

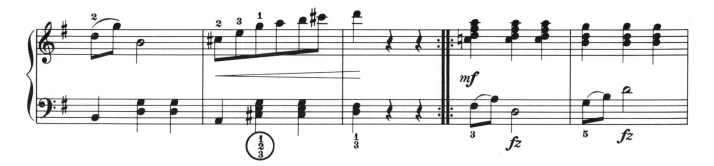

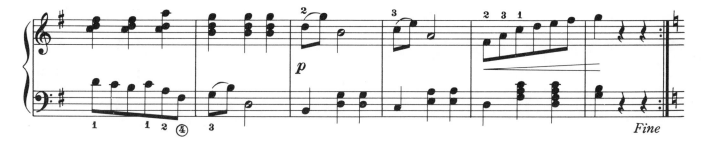

Fine

Trio

D.C.

Waltz

Fritz Spindler

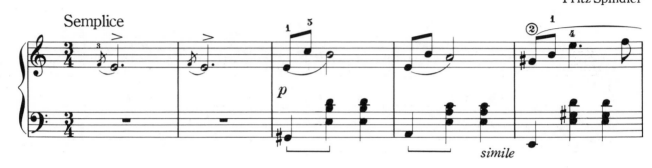

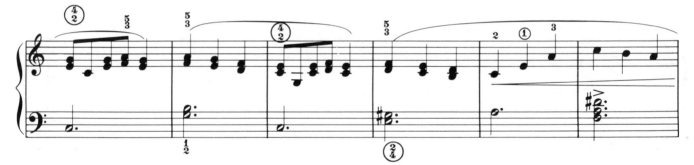

Sad Story

George Becker

Allegretto

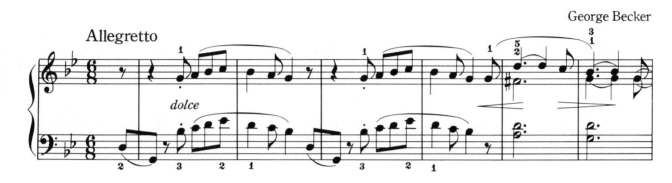

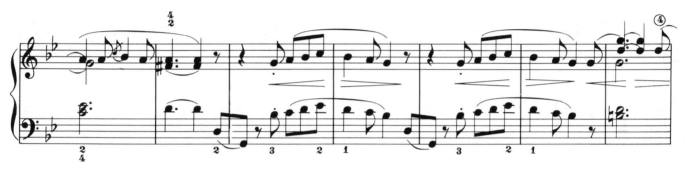

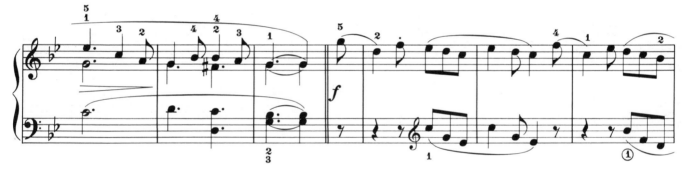

March

Allegro

Tempo di marcia

Ignaz Moscheles

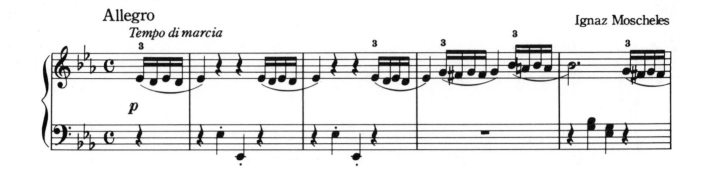

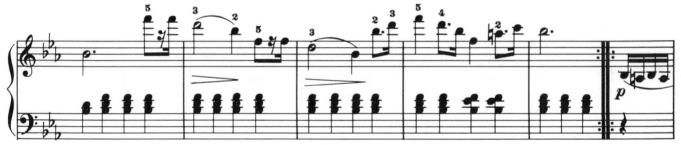

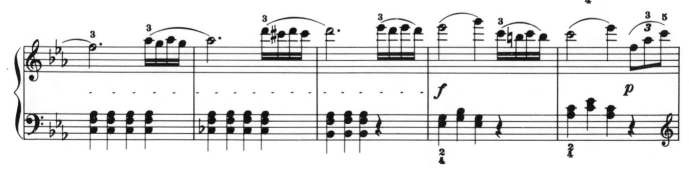

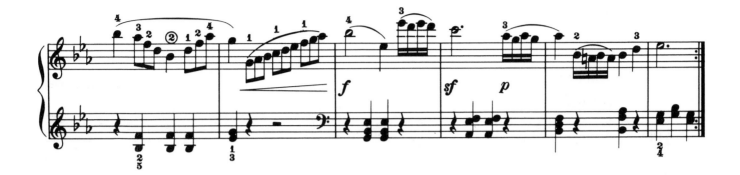

Prelude

Georges Bizet

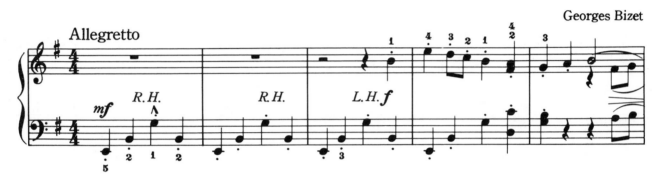

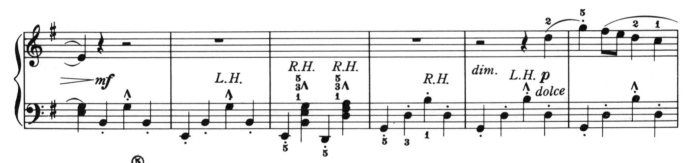

Grisen

Edvard Grieg

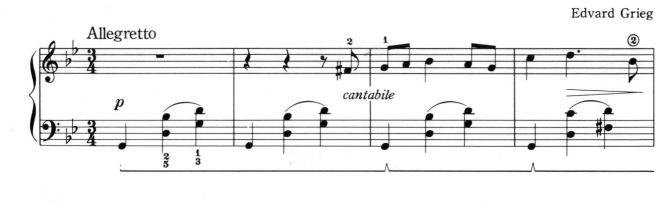

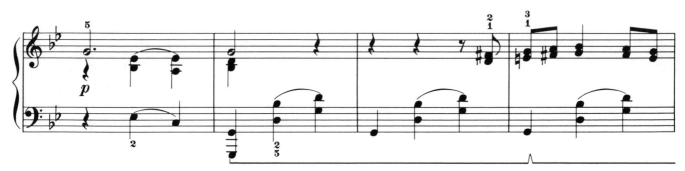

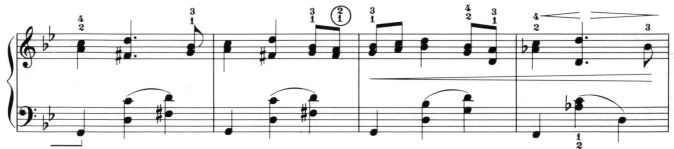

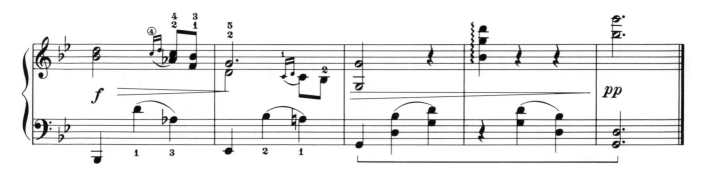

The Organ Grinder

Peter I. Tchaikovsky

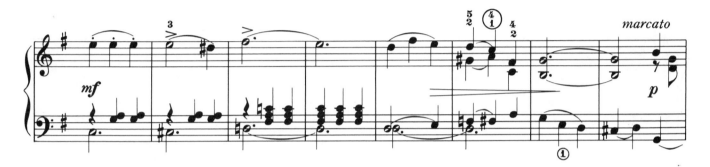

Clowns

Dmitri Kabalevsky

ETUDES

Careful fingering for continuous flow of semiquavers, 50

Equal demisemiquavers and demisemiquaver rests, 59

Four-voice chords played legato with careful use of pedal, 44

Grace notes, careful listening required for graceful balance in alternating hands, 53

Left hand solo with running figure in semiquavers, 54

Legato melody in one hand, a non-legato chord in the other, 42

Maintaining tempo although changed rhythmic figure and change in Major to Minor, 58

Many details – requires diligent work to bring out qualities in this piece, 57

Melody of two-bar phrases, crescendo and diminuendo, 55

Melody with off-beat accents and repeated chord accompaniment, 46

Motivic development, right hand, left hand, 60

Phrasing of melodic legato scale-figures, 43

Semiquavers superimposed on a firm crotchet beat, 56

Smooth-flowing harmonic left hand accompaniment, 52

To develop touch accuracy in staccato broken octaves, 45

Variety of touches in right hand, 48

Bertini, Henri (French) 1789-1876
Burgmüller, Friedrich (German) 1806-1874
Concone, Joseph (Italian) 1810-1861
Czerny, Carl (Austrian) 1791-1857
Gurlitt, Cornelius (German) 1820-1901
Hässler, Johann Wilhelm (German) 1747-1822
Le Couppey, Félix (French) 1811-1887
Lemoine, Henri (French) 1786-1854
Spindler, Fritz (German) 1817-1905

Legato melody in one hand, a non-legato chord in the other

Fritz Spindler

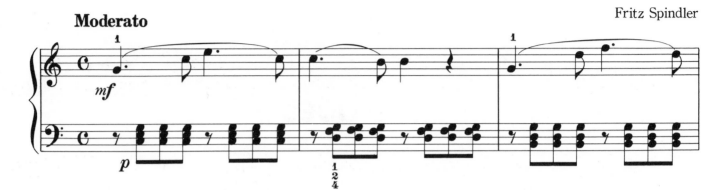

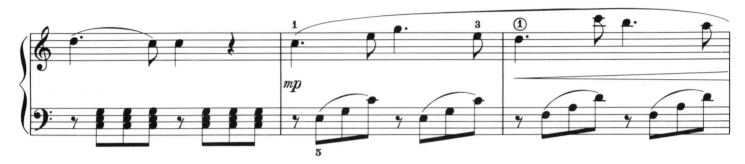

Phrasing of melodic legato scale-figures

Johann Wilhelm Hässler

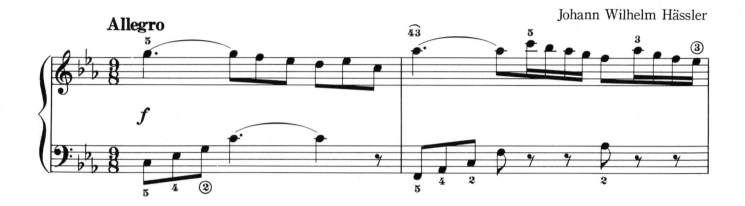

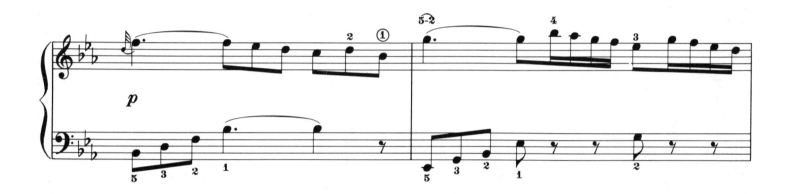

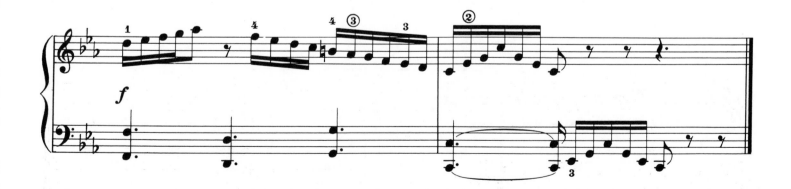

Four-voice chords played legato with careful use of pedal

Henri Bertini

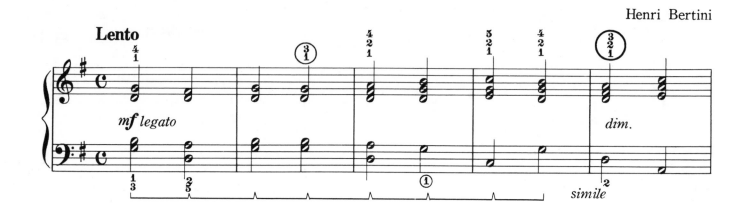

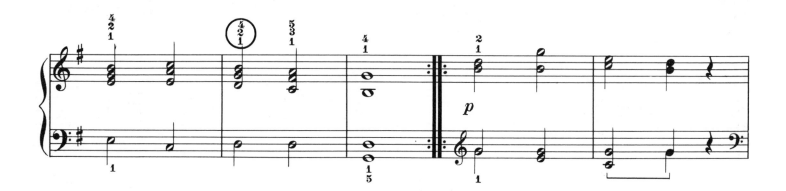

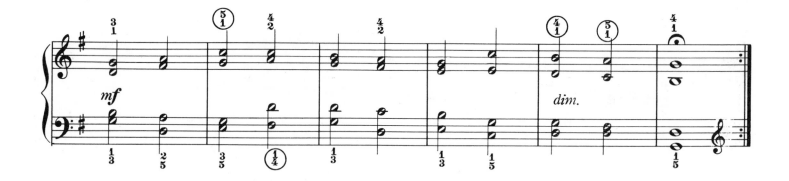

To develop touch accuracy in staccato broken octaves

Henri Bertini

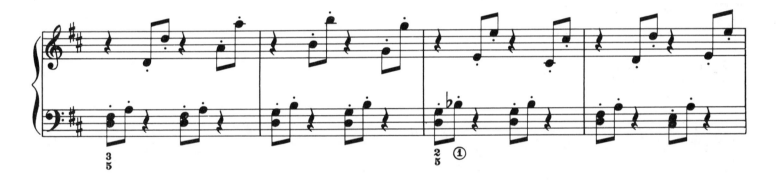

46

Melody with off-beat accents and repeated chord accompaniment

Carl Czerny

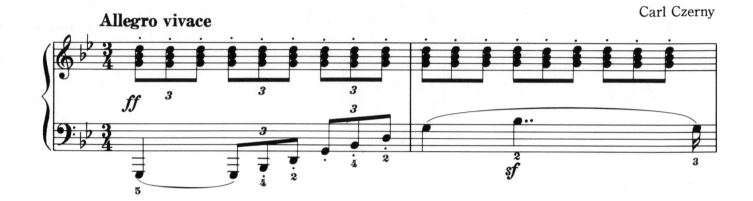

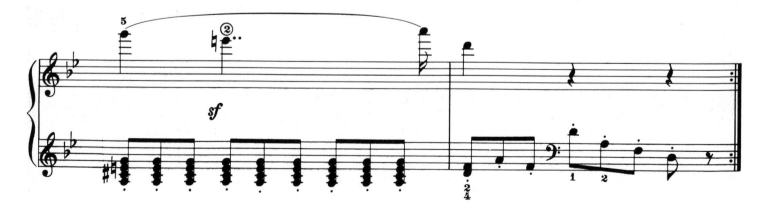

Variety of touches in right hand

Henri Lemoine

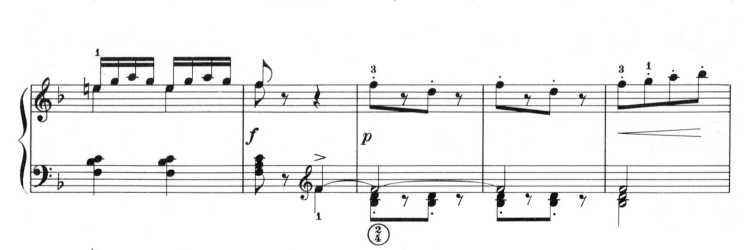

Careful fingering for continuous flow of semiquavers

Cornelius Gurlitt

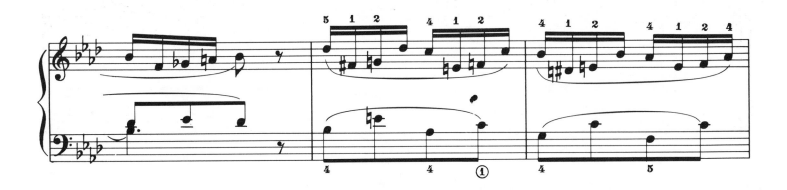

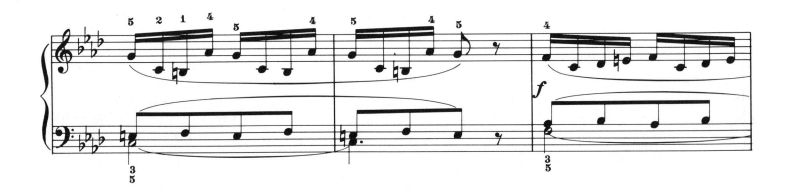

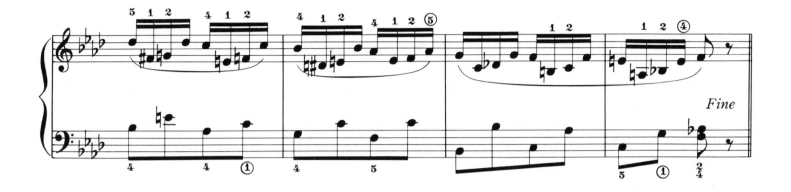

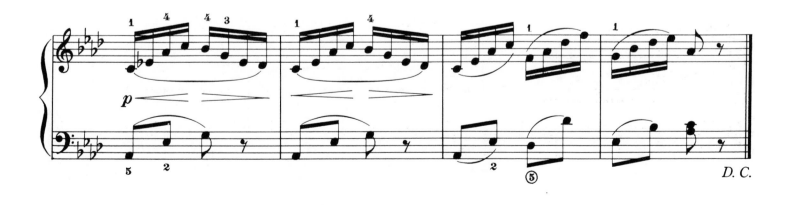

Smooth-flowing harmonic left hand accompaniment

Fritz Spindler

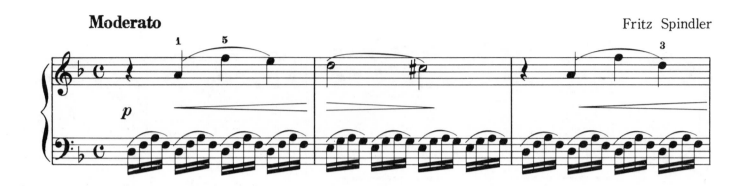

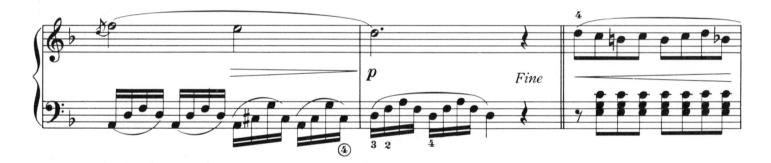

D. C.

Grace notes, careful listening required
for graceful balance in alternating hands

Carl Czerny

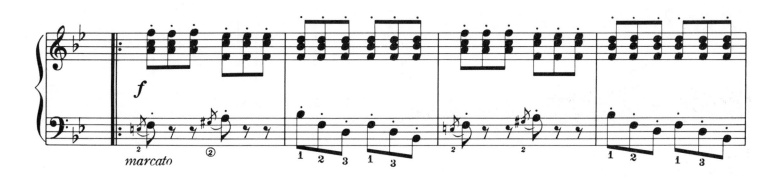

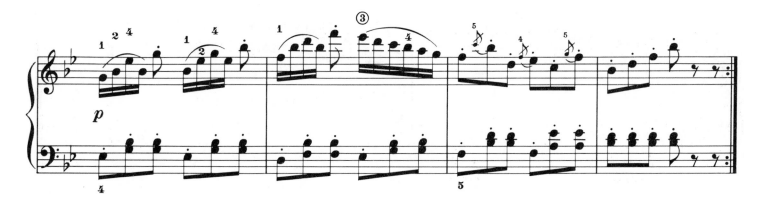

Left hand solo with running figure in semiquavers

Joseph Concone

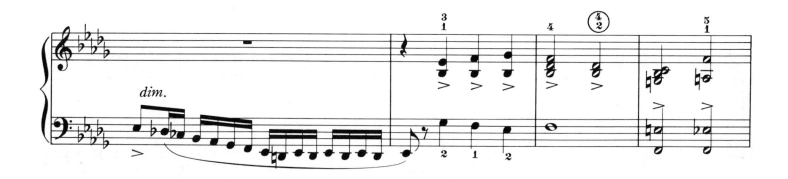

Melody of two-bar phrases, crescendo and diminuendo

Félix Le Couppey

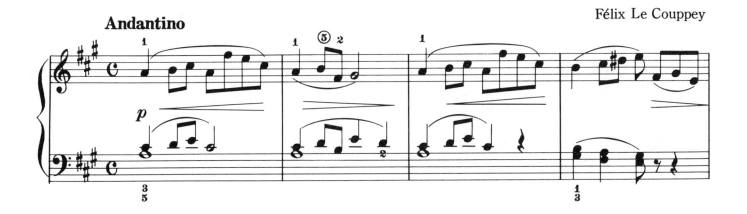

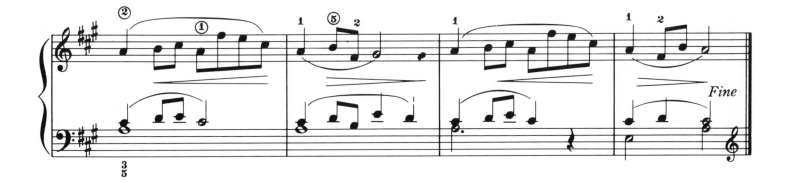

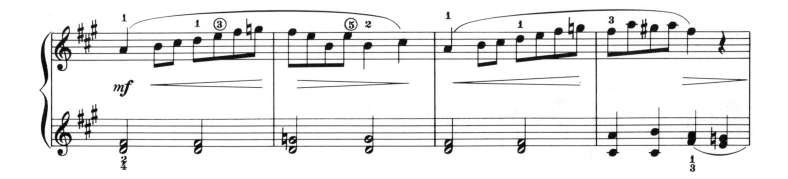

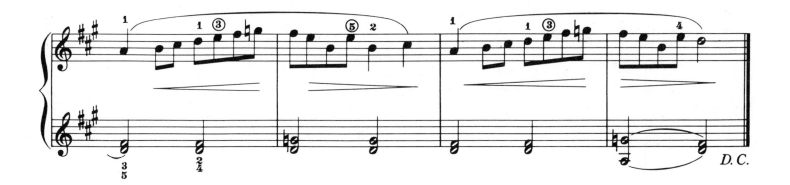

55

Semiquavers superimposed on a firm crochet beat

Friedrich Burgmüller

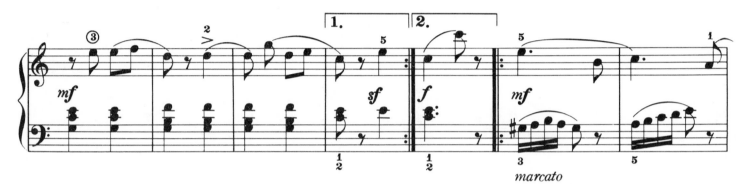

Many details – requires diligent work
to bring out qualities in this piece

Carl Czerny

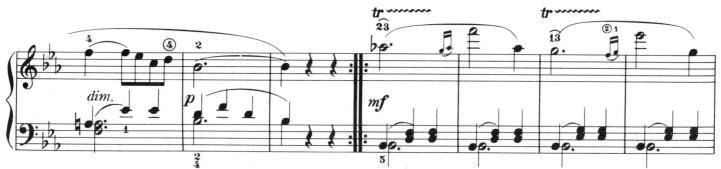

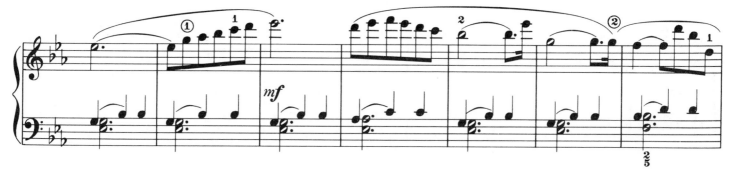

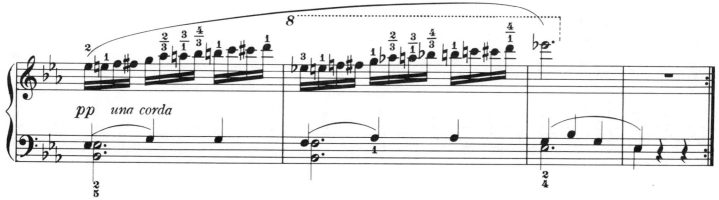

Maintaining tempo although changed rhythmic figure
and change in Major to Minor

Johann Wilhelm Hässler

Allegro assai

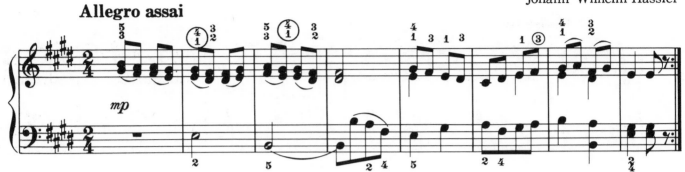

Da capo Maggiore

Equal demisemiquavers and demisemiquaver rests

Carl Czerny

Allgretto

Motivic development, right hand, left hand

Johann Wilhelm Hässler

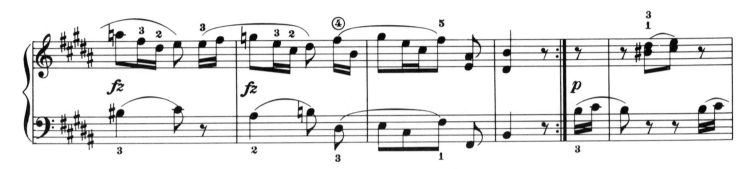

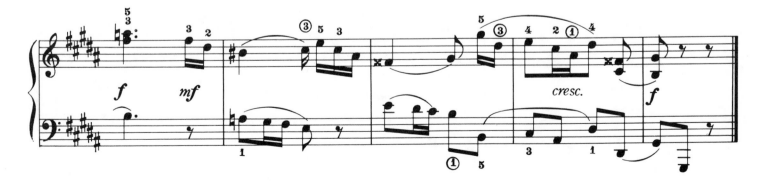

SONATINAS

Johann Anton André – Sonatina, Op.34, No.3, 72

Domenico Cimarosa – Sonata, 64

Antonio Diabelli – Sonatina, Op.168, No.1, 76

George Frideric Handel – Fantasia, 62

Wolfgang Amadeus Mozart – Viennese Sonata, 66

André, Johann Anton (German) 1775-1842
Cimarosa, Domenico (Italian) 1749-1801
Diabelli, Antonio (Austrian) 1781-1858
Handel, George Frideric (German) 1685-1759
Mozart, Wolfgang Amadeus (Austrian) 1756-1791

Fantasia

George Frideric Handel

Allegro

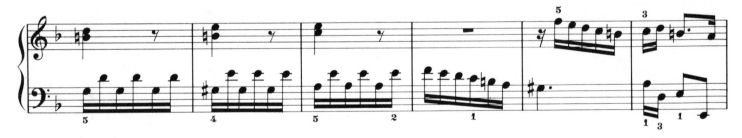

Sonata

Andantino

Domenico Cimarosa

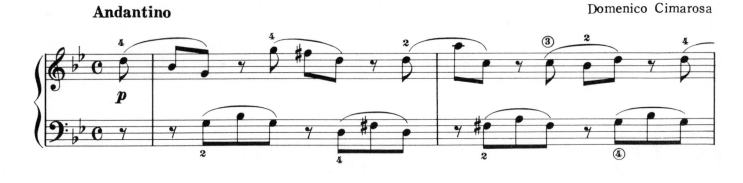

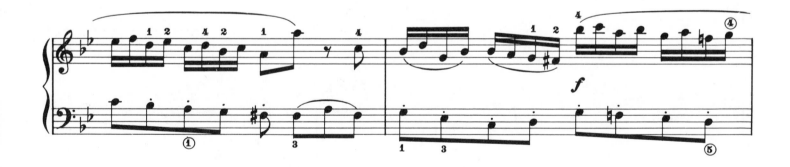

Viennese Sonata

Andante grazioso

Wolfgang Amadeus Mozart

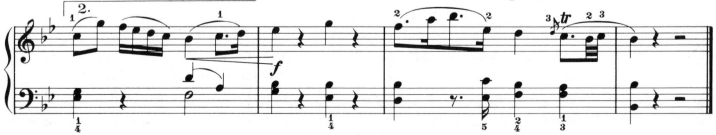

Menuetto
Allegretto

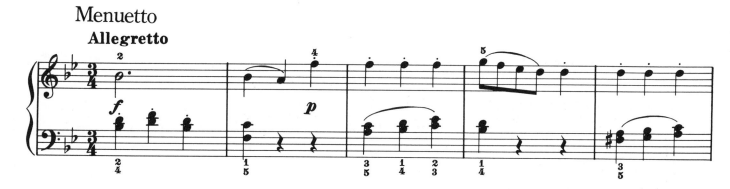

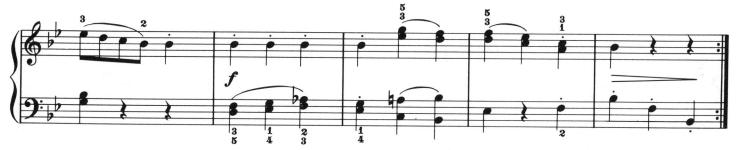

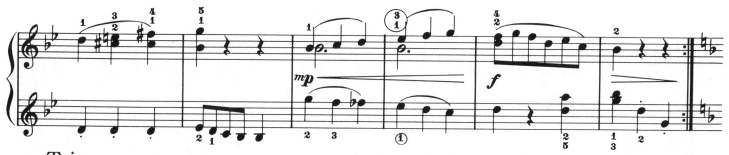

Trio

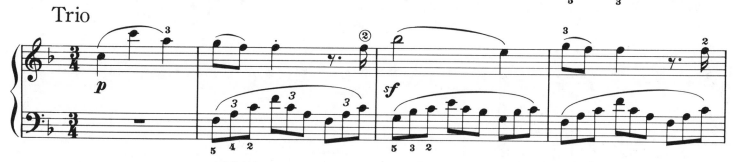

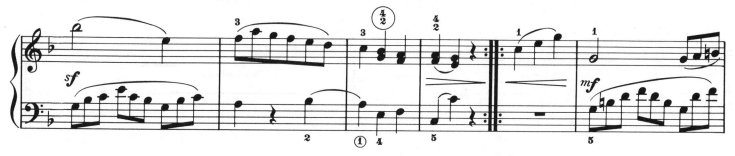

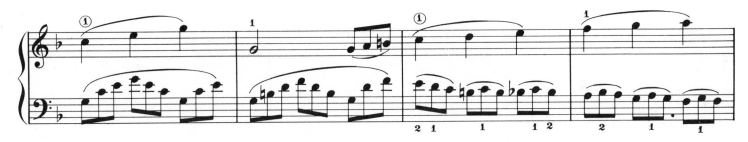

Menuetto da Capo

Rondo
Allegro

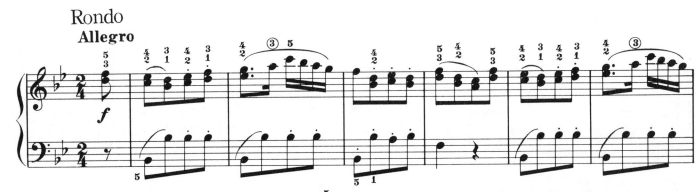

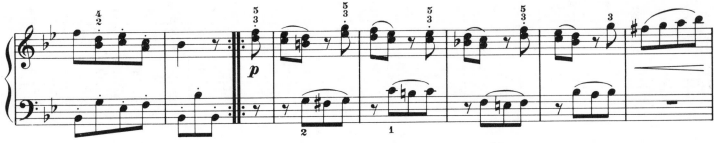

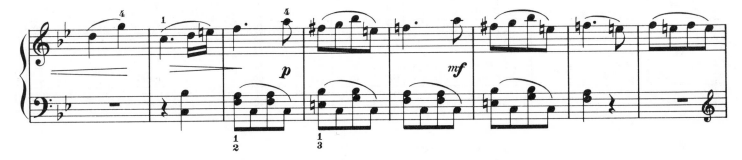

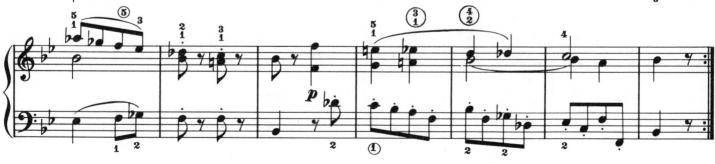

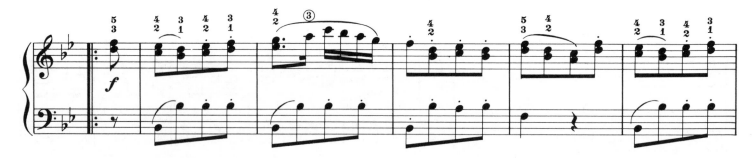

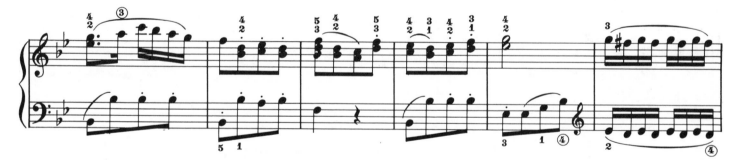

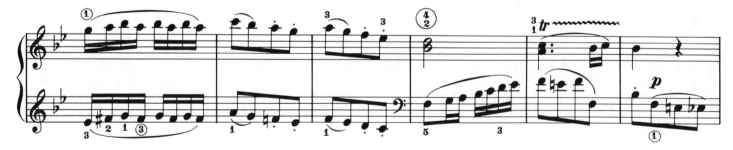

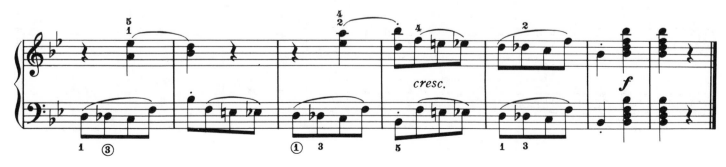

Sonatina
(Op.34, No.3)

Johann Anton André

Moderato

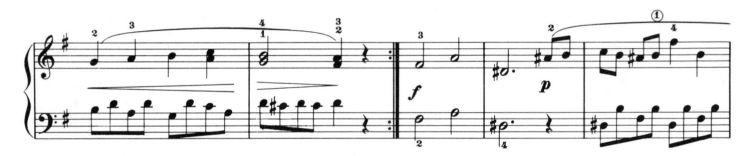

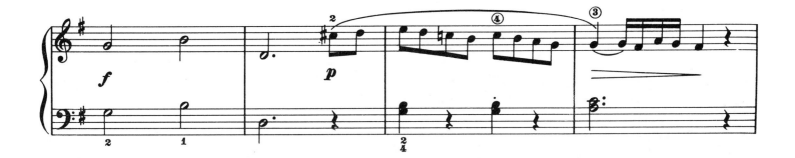

Rondo
Allegretto

Sonatina

(Op.168, No.1)

Antonio Diabelli

Moderato cantabile

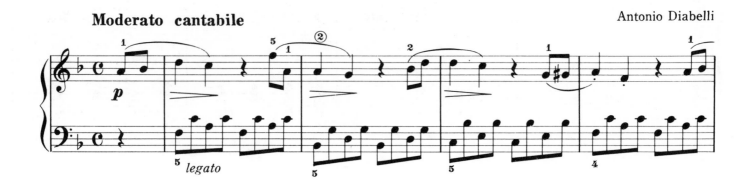

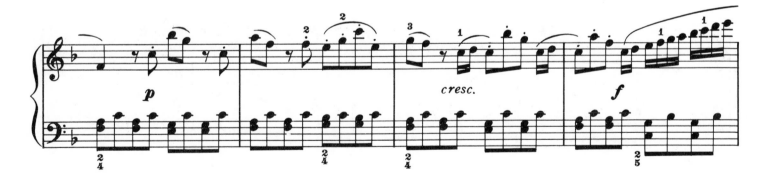

Andante cantabile

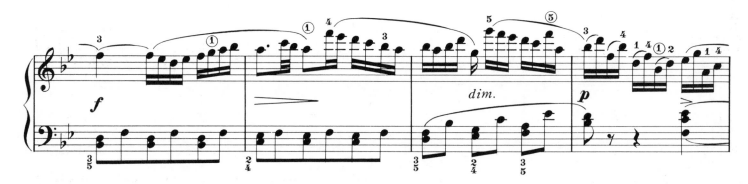

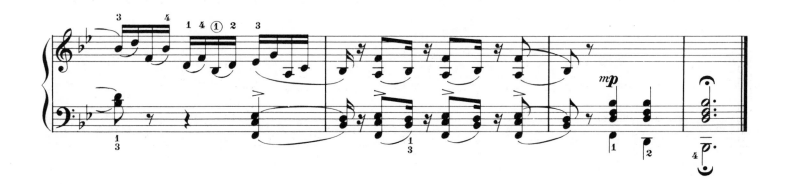

Rondo
Allegretto

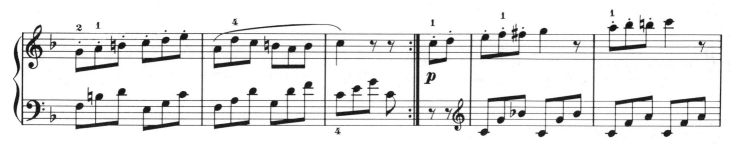

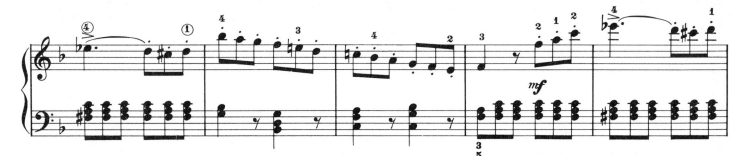

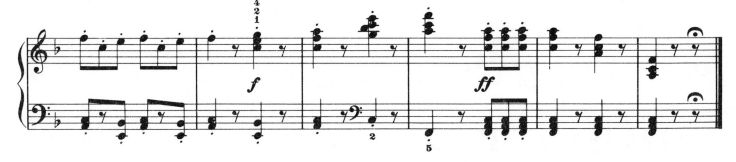

DUETS

Anton Arensky – Tears, 92

Adolphe Blanc – Scherzetto, 88

Franz Schubert – Ländler, 86

Peter I. Tchaikovsky – On The Meadow, 92

Daniel G. Türk – The Storm, 82

Arensky, Anton (Russian) 1861-1906
Blanc, Adolphe (French) 1828-1885
Schubert, Franz (Austrian) 1797-1828
Tchaikovsky, Peter Ilyich (Russian) 1840-1893
Türk, Daniel Gottlob (German) 1756-1813

The Storm

Secondo

Daniel G. Türk

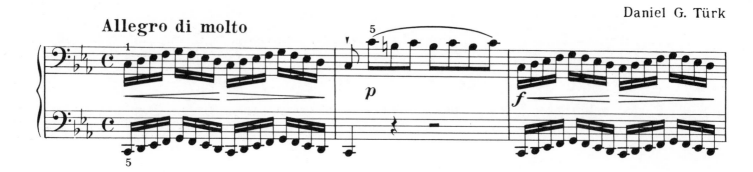

The Storm

Primo

Daniel G. Türk

Allegro di molto

A

B

1.

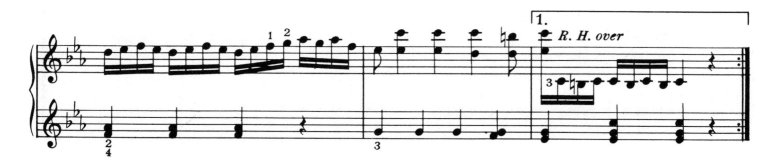

Secondo

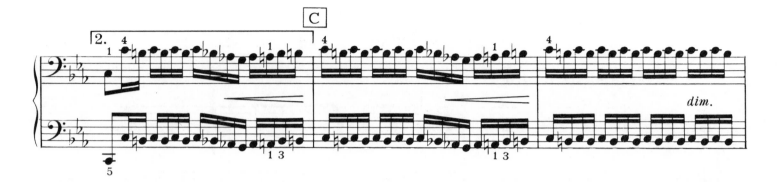

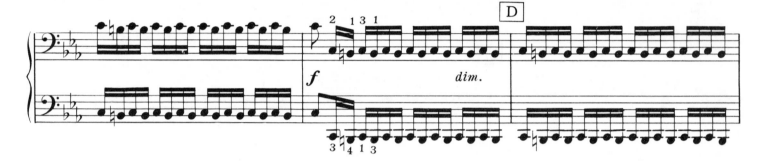

Allegretto grazioso All of a sudden the sky is clear

Primo

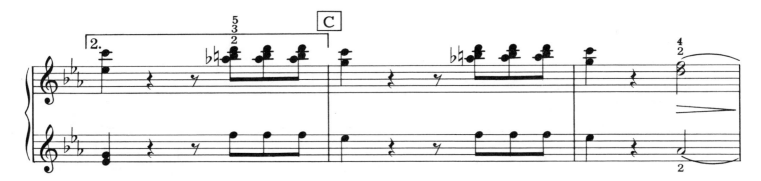

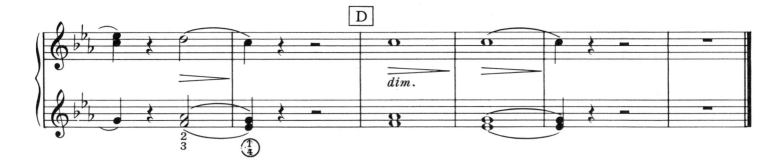

Allegretto grazioso All of a sudden the sky is clear

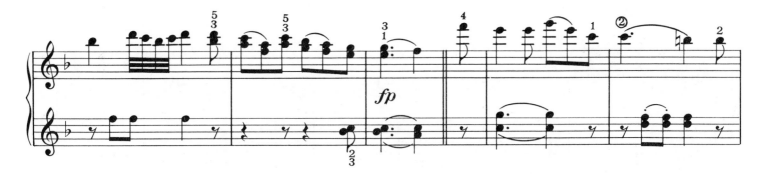

Ländler

Secondo

Moderato

Franz Schubert

Ländler

Primo

Franz Schubert

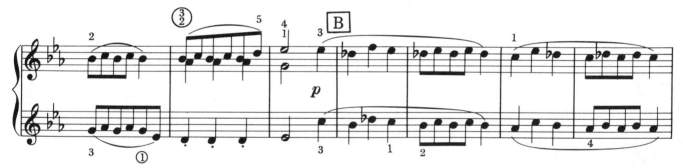

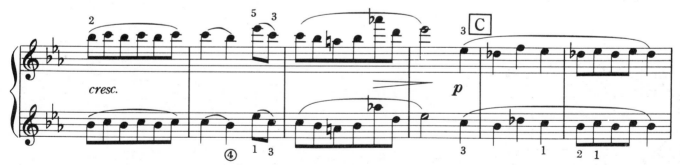

Scherzetto

Secondo

Adolphe Blanc

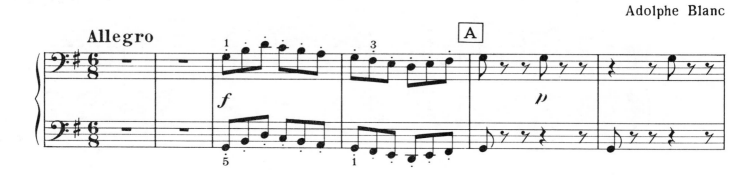

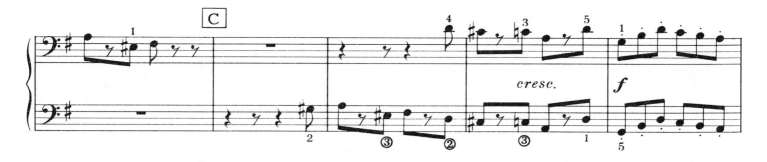

Scherzetto

Primo

Adolphe Blanc

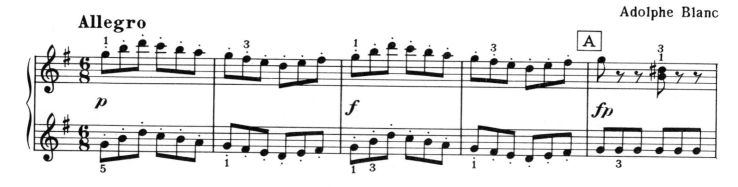

Secondo

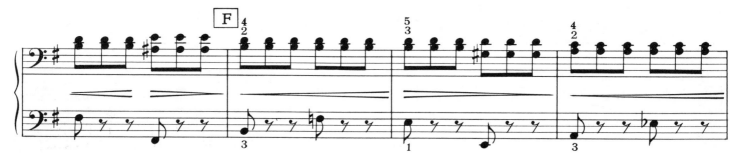

Da Capo poi la Coda

Primo

Trio

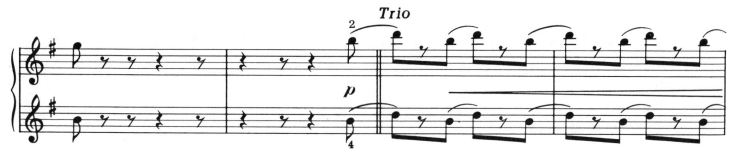

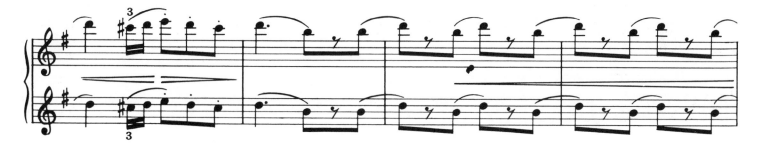

Coda

Da Capo poi la Coda

On The Meadow

Secondo

Peter I. Tchaikovsky

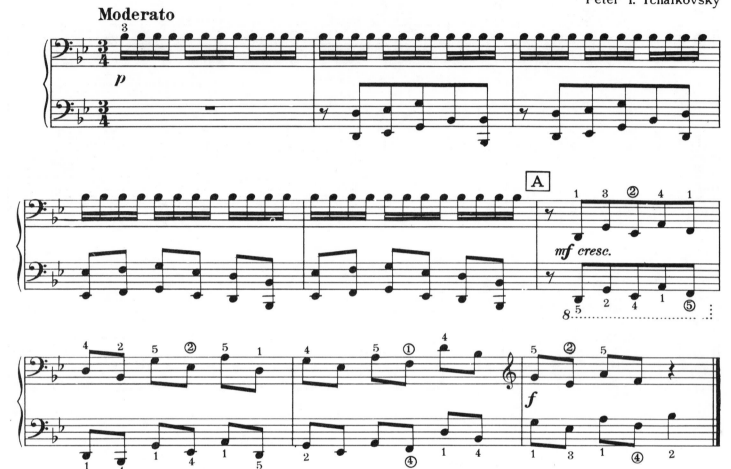

Tears

Anton Arensky

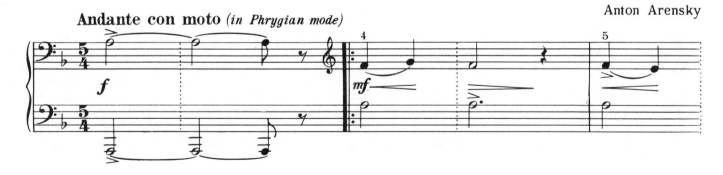

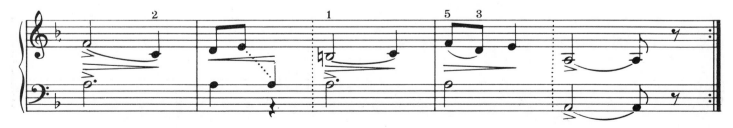

On The Meadow

Primo

Peter I. Tchaikovsky

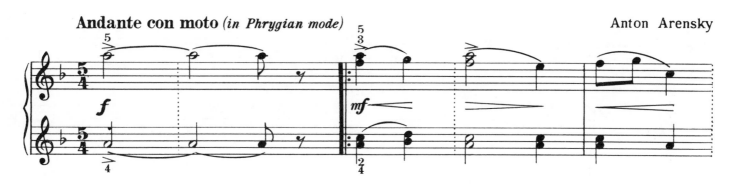

Tears

Anton Arensky

94

Secondo

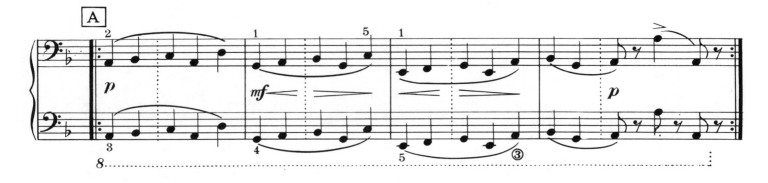

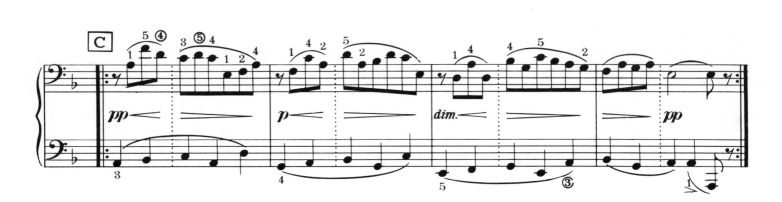

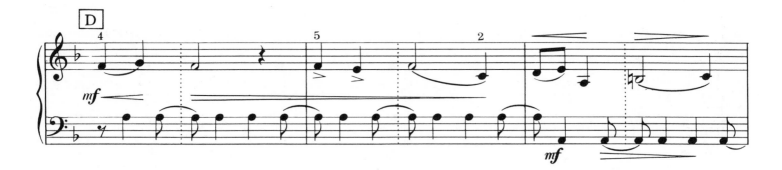

Primo

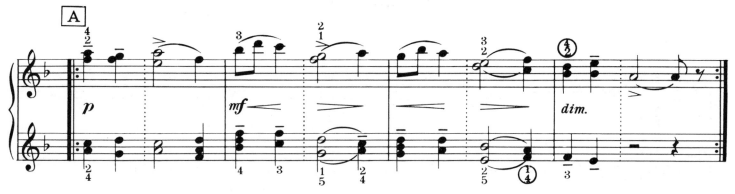

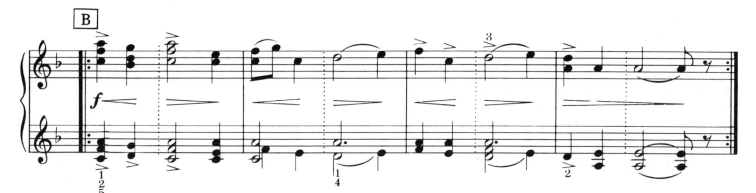

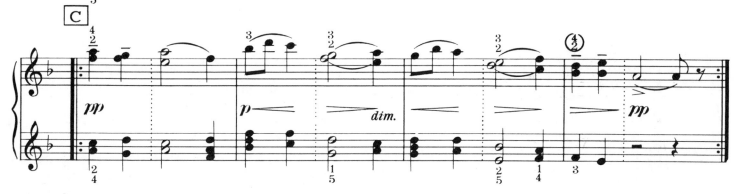

GLOSSARY

adagio — *slow*
agitato — *agitated*
a l'istesso tempo — *at same speed*
allegretto — *rather lively*
allegro — *rather slow*
andantino — *a little faster than andante*
a tempo — *at the original speed*
assai — *very, rather*
Bagatelle — *a trifle, light musical piece*
ben marcato — *well marked, brought out*
cantabile — *singing*
coda — *section at end of piece*
con grazia — *with grace*
con moto — *with motion*
cresc., crescendo — *gradually getting louder*
D.C., da capo al fine — *return to the beginning*
then play the Coda
decresc., decrescendo —*gradually getting softer*
dim., diminuendo —*gradually getting softer*
di molto — *much, very*
dolce — *sweetly*
e — *and*
Ecossaise — *lively Scottish dance* $\frac{2}{4}$ *time*
fine — *the end*
Gigue — *a jig, lively dance*
giocoso — *happily, playfully*
grazioso — *gracefully*
Ländler — *dance in* $\frac{3}{4}$ *, related to the Waltz*
L.H. — *left hand*
legato —   *connected, bound together*
leggiero   — *lightly*

lento — *slow*
ma — *but*
Maggiore — *major, section in major key*
marcato — *to be brought out*
Mazurka — *Polish dance in* $\frac{3}{4}$
meno mosso — *slower*
Minuet — *slow, stately dance in* $\frac{3}{4}$
moderato — *at moderate speed*
non troppo — *not too much*
poco — *a little*
poco a poco — *little by little*
presto — *very fast*
rall., rallentando — *gradually getting slower*
R.H. — *right hand*
risoluto — *resolved, in a decided manner*
Rondo — *in which principal section is repeated*
several times in same key with interludes
in different keys
schalkhaft — *playfully*
schnell — *fast*
semplice — *simply*
simile — *the same*
tempo di marcia — *in March time*
tempo prima — *at the original speed*
tranquillo — *tranquilly, quietly*
Trio — *secondary section in a Minuet*
or certain other dances
vivace — *lively, quite fast*
vivo — *lively*
Waltz — *dance in* $\frac{3}{4}$

getting louder

crescendo fork

pp	*p*	*mp*	*mf*	*f*	*ff*
pianissimo	piano	mezzo piano	mezzo forte	forte	fortissimo
(*pyah NISS e mo*)	(*PYAH no*)	(*MED zo PYAH no*)	(*MED zo FOR te*)	(*FOR te*)	(*for TISS e mo*)

fermata (*fehr MAH tah*)
pause, hold

> —accent mark

tr - trill sign

diminuendo fork—getting softer

sf, fz
sforzato (*sfort SAH to*)
a strong accent

—hold for full time value

//
cesura—a complete separation

—repeat sign

fp
forte piano (*FOR teh PYAH no*)
loud on the individual
note or chord and then soft

notes to be held as long as possible
but then repeated. not tied

Λ —a heavy accent